Dist

from

Loved

Ones

Other books by James Tate

The Lost Pilot

The Oblivion Ha-Ha

Hints to Pilgrims

Absences

Hottentot Ossuary

Viper Jazz

Riven Doggeries

Constant Defender

Reckoner

Wesleyan University Press

Published by University Press of New England

Hanover and London

Distance from Loved Ones

James Tate

Some of these poems originally appeared in *Caliban, Denver Quarterly, Grand Street, Harvard Book Review, The Iowa Review, The Massachusetts Review, New Letters, Ploughshares,* and *The Village Voice*; "Quabbin Reservoir," "The Condemned Man," "Bewitched," "A Little Skull," "How Was Your Day?," "Saturdays Are for Bathing Betsy," "'Burn Down the Town, No Survivors,'" "The Banner," "Editor," "Pastoral," "You Are My Destination and Desire, Fading," and "Indivisible" in *American Poetry Review*; "Trying to Help," "City at Night," "Nuisance," "No Spitting Up" in *Poetry.*

Printed in the United States of America

∞

Library of Congress Cataloging-in-Publication Data
Tate, James, 1943–
Distance from loved ones / James Tate.
p. cm. — (Wesleyan poetry)
ISBN 0–8195–2189–2 (alk. paper) — ISBN 0–8195–1191–9 (pbk. : alk. paper)
I. Title. II. Series.
PS3570.A8D5 1990
811′.54—dc20 89–70659
CIP

WESLEYAN POETRY

5 4 3 2 1

For Charles and Charles

Contents

I

Instead of learning to live
a loving life,
people learn how to fly.
They fly very badly,
but they stop learning
to live lovingly in order
to learn how to fly
after a fashion.
It is just as if
birds stopped flying
and tried learning to run
or build bicycles
and ride on them.

—Leo Tolstoy,
Diary for Myself Alone

Quabbin Reservoir

All morning, skipping stones on the creamy lake,
I thought I heard a lute being played, high up,
in the birch trees, or a faun speaking French
with a Brooklyn accent. A snowy owl watched me
with half-closed eyes. "What have you done for me
philately," I wanted to ask, licking the air.
There was a village at the bottom of the lake,
and I could just make out the old post office,
and, occasionally, when the light struck it just right,
I glimpsed several mailmen swimming in or out of it,
letters and packages escaping randomly, 1938, 1937,
it didn't matter to them any longer. *Void.*
No such address. Soft blazes squirmed across the surface
and I could see their church, now home to druid squatters,
rock in the intoxicating current, as if to an ancient hymn.
And a thousand elbowing reeds conducted the drowsy band pavilion:
awake, awake, you germs of habit! Alas, I fling
my final stone, my calling card, my gift of porphyry
to the citizens of the deep, and disappear into a copse,
raving like a butterfly to a rosebud: I love you.

Peggy in the Twilight

Peggy spent half of each day trying to wake up, and
the other half preparing for sleep. Around five, she
would mix herself something preposterous and '40s-ish
like a Grasshopper or a Brass Monkey, adding a note
of gaiety to her defeat. This shadowlife became her.
She always had a glow on; that is, she carried an aura
of innocence as well as death with her.

I first met her at a party almost thirty years ago.
Even then it was too late for tragic women, tragic
anything. Still, when she was curled up and fell asleep
in the corner, I was overwhelmed with feelings of love.
Petite black and gold angels sat on her slumped shoulders
and sang lullabies to her.

I walked into another room and asked our host for
a blanket for Peggy.

"Peggy?" he said. "There's no one here by that name."

And so my lovelife began.

Distance from Loved Ones

After her husband died, Zita decided to get the face-lift
she had always wanted. Halfway through the operation
her blood pressure started to drop, and they had to stop.
When Zita tried to fasten her seat belt for her sad drive
home, she threw out her shoulder. Back at the hospital
the doctor examined her and found cancer run rampant
throughout her shoulder and arm and elsewhere. Radiation
followed. And, now, Zita just sits there in her beauty parlor,
bald, crying and crying.

My mother tells me all this on the phone, and I say:
Mother, who is Zita?

And my mother says, I am Zita. All my life I have been
Zita, bald and crying. And you, my son, who should have known
me best, thought I was nothing but your mother.

But, Mother, I say, I am dying. . . .

The Condemned Man

The condemned man clutches his lucky penny.
He paces the park, famished, recounting
incurable injuries, condemning the scoundrel
in him, banishing the swindler, pleading
with his jury to show no mercy. The grocer
watches from his doorway, recoiling from
the dreary display—he has goat cheese and radishes
to consider, turnips under intense surveillance.
A limousine squeezes through the traffic,
smothering the thoughts of little people.
An errand boy percolates down the sidewalk,
cracking codes in his mind, lumping forecasts
and rituals into sure treasure by tomorrow.
A plump and dusky woman with something on a leash
pauses to inspect some loaves and peppers,
licking her lips and speaking a private language
to her nervous pet, who's ready to croak.
"Fiber, Mrs. Zumstein, fiber's the only thing!"
the grocer quips, swatting flies from the lumpy morsels.
And, across the street, a net is dropped from the trees.
Men in blue costumes fan-out and sweep through the park.
Dogs pick up a scent in the breeze and dash yapping
over the ridge, where, in their teeming zest,
they upend a baby carriage and frighten a young mother
nearly to death. The condemned man briskly apologizes
to his condemned god and withdraws from the park quietly.

Bewitched

I was standing in the lobby,
some irritant in my eye,
thinking back on a soloist
I once heard in Venezuela,
and then, for some reason,
on a crate of oranges recently
arrived from a friend in Florida,
and then this colleague came up to me
and asked me what time it was,
and I don't know what came over me
but I was certain that I was standing there naked
and I was certain she could see my thoughts,
so I tried to hide them quickly,
I was embarrassed that there was
no apparent connection to them,
will-o'-the-wisps, and I needed an alibi,
so I told her I had seen a snapshot
of a murder victim recently
that greatly resembled her,
and that she should take precaution,
my intonation getting me into deeper trouble
and I circled the little space I had cut out
as if looking for all the sidereal years
she had inquired into moments before,
and the dazzling lunar poverty of some thoughts
had me pinned like a moth
and my dubious tactic to hide my malady
had prompted this surreptitious link
to the whirling Sufi dancers,
once so popular in these halls.
"It's five minutes past four," I said,
knowing I had perjured myself for all time.
I veered into the men's room,
astonished to have prevailed,
my necktie, a malediction stapled in place,
my zipper synchronized with the feminine motive.
In Zagreb, just now, a hunter is poaching some cherries.

Saturdays Are for Bathing Betsy

I am thinking about Betsy almost all the time now.
I am also thinking about the relationship between
a man and his watch. I am amazed at how each sort
of animal and plant manages to keep its kind alive.
Shocking poultry. Maybe there's a movie playing
downtown about a dotty fat woman with a long knife
who dismembers innocent ducks and chickens. But it
is the reconstruction of the villa of the mysteries
that is killing me. How each sort of animal and
plant prevents itself from returning to dust
just a little while longer while I transfer some
assets to a region where there are no thinking creatures,
just worshipping ones. They oscillate along like magicians,
deranged seaweed fellows and their gals, a Nile landscape
littered with Pygmies. I'm lolling on the banks.
I am not just a bunch of white stuff inside my skull.
No, there is this villa, and in the villa there is
a bathing pool, and on Saturdays Betsy always visits.
I am not the first rational man, but my tongue
does resemble a transmitter. And, when wet, she
is a triangle. And when she's wet, time has a fluff-
iness about it, and that has me trotting about,
loathing any locomotion not yoked to her own.

How Happy We Were

There was a spy in my life who wouldn't let me sleep.
Day in and day out she tortured me with the most sophisticated
devices. At first I squealed like a pig at slaughter.
Then I became addicted. Between sessions I was agitated
and impatient. I cried, "How much longer must I wait?"
So she made me wait longer and longer. I became masterful,
a genius of the thumbscrew and rack. I didn't really need her
any longer. On her last visit she could read this in my eyes,
and it tore a hole in her through which I could see
something like eternity and a few of the little angels
whose sole job it is to fake weeping for people like us.

Consolations After an Affair

My plants are whispering to one another:
they are planning a little party
later on in the week about watering time.
I have quilts on beds and walls
that think it is still the 19th century.
They know nothing of automobiles and jet planes.
For them a wheat field in January
is their mother and enough.
I've discovered that I don't need
a retirement plan, a plan to succeed.
A snow leopard sleeps beside me
like a slow, warm breeze.
And I can hear the inner birds singing
alone in this house I love.

"Burn Down the Town, No Survivors"

Those were my orders,
issued with a sense of rightness
I'd rarely known. I was tired
of how June was treating John,
how Mary was victimizing herself
with nearly everyone, Mark
was a loose cannon, and Carlotta
would never find any peace.
It seemed to me that there could be
no acceptable resolution for anyone,
except those who didn't deserve one.
And when, for a moment, I held the power,
I surveyed the landscape—it was
just a typical mid-sized town
in the middle of nowhere—and
the citizens showed no signs
of remorse, as if what they were doing
to one another (and to me) was
what we were here for (and I recognize
the mistake in that kind of thinking,
but still . . .) a bold and decisive action
seemed so appealing, even healing.
I was with a friend's wife, her
wild mane would make such ideal kindling—
I could have loved her but it would
have been just more of the same,
more petty crimes and slow death,
more passion leading to betrayal,
more ecstasy guaranteeing tears. I saw
how dangerous and fragile I had become.
I could have loved a fig right then
with my gasoline in one hand,

and the other fluttering between
her breast and a packet of matches.
My contagious laughter frightening us both,
"No survivors," I repeated, and
we looked through one another,
the work already completed.

City at Night

The blueblack plumes of the fountain
parched my yearning, and a tuft of cellophane
clings fondly to my foot like a diadem.
Down that street an uproar is dwindling,
a small word had been magnified and was
once again shrinking back to its reasonable size,
and Joe Blow drifts down to the riverbank
searching for relics, a man of sorrows.
Then a new turmoil infects another flock;
it's a good corner on which to sell balm.
A seer bobs along, oblivious or beguiled.
I look for my reflection in a window:
Good night Joe, Good night Joe, Good night.

A Little Skull

I found a skull on the beach,
it was just a little skull,
maybe that of a canary.
White sand trickled through the sockets.
It seemed to smile at me
and I tried feeding it some crumbs.
Oh well, cookies are for frogs,
and maybe this isn't a skull at all,
but an egg or a bulb of some sort.
Maybe I will glue some sequins on it
and donate it to the local monastery.
It would be happy there, supervising
the luncheon menu, pounding its forehead
through the lilac sermons, patrolling
the starched brainwaves in the library.
But what if it's my own long-lost ancestor?
Shouldn't I guzzle a toast about now?
Raise a kite, or faint in a spiral upward?
The whole episode is lamentable, I'm simply
rehearsing for another kind of scrutiny,
an expedition into the heart of heresy
where dowdy, abusive hobgoblins lounge
yanking at one another's hair and snapping
newcomers with hot towels. I expect
to be incarcerated there for some time.
All nectar will taste like insecticide.
Privileges, such as holding this bird's skull
in the palm of my hand, will surely be rare.
And so, better to forfeit it now, savor forever
its twirling arc back into the sea, and circulate
among the clustered natives, sniffing for honey,
whisking flies from laughing faces.

Under Mounting Pressure

"O Marcel," she says to me, "O Marcel,
do you know the way out of this pool?
I am very tired of swimming about here."
A gale from her shoulder left me in dishabille.
I was in dishabille anyway as I was just back
from the kaleidoscopic society.
I was just there to salute her as she passed.
She was a floating beautyfarm.
I had planned to escort her to the demolition derby.
She was a floating beautyfarm
and I stood there on the wharf of the final landing.
She recognized me as some Marcel-type of guy—
this was incomprehensible to me, but preparatory
to something perhaps worthwhile.
A quizzical, if concupiscent smile exhausted itself in my head
and I stretched out my hand, the Grand Mogul I really was.
I started reeling in this wildcat beautyfarm,
it was a big one. Her ledger of love was a blur,
her helmet was full of holes. "O Marcel," she said to me,
"O Marcel, there's a doorbell in your head. Don't touch it!"

Certain Nuances, Certain Gestures

The way a lady
entertaining an illicit desire touches her earlobe
in a crowded room, and the way that room seems to single
her out and undress her with murmuring torchlight—
if the right spectator is present, even though the
band is playing loudly and the myriad celebrants
are toasting their near-tragic rise to glory, and the
Vice President of an important bank is considering
an assassination, and even the mice in the boiler room
are planning a raid on an old bag of cookies in the
attic—even so, this spectator senses the moisture
on her palms, can feel her thoughts wander in and out
of the cavernous room; knows, too, their approximate
destination. Beyond this, he refuses to follow.
She stands alone there on the quay, waiting. The
river of life is flowing. The spectator returns
to his room, a few hours closer to his own death
or ecstasy. He makes a few hasty entries into his
diary before turning off the light. And, yes, he dreams,
but of a gazelle frozen in the path of a runaway truck.

Mimi

After the train wreck
I found her hat
in the top branches of a catalpa tree.
It was all feathers,
green and pink and blue,
and it shivered in my hands
like a starveling from Fiji
too happy or frightened
to remember its way home.
Oh, it's true, she drank too much champagne
on all the wrong occasions.
She hired a limousine
when she could have crawled.
Her laughter made me freeze,
and when she exposed her breast
I was a Naval Cadet
about to leave for a losing war.
"Something to die for," she said.
And I did, every night, every day.
I told her not to take this train,
puzzle of hot steel
beside the river we never swam.
But there was something out there
that she needed more than me.
So she donned her hat of tragic feathers
and vanished from this life.
And I am left in the present
with a history that could never matter.
I know what day it is, what hour,
and I see many strangers
whose Christmases did not work out,
who broke under the pressure.
And the frozen hare over there,
isn't he some kind of freedom fighter?
Tribulations over rations.
A hat that wants to fly to the moon.

You Are My Destination and Desire, Fading

Dawn animal, why don't you come out now
and have a nice cuppa?
I am reading the obituaries, strenuously,
which is what one does to get ready.
I am counting the fissures in my egg.
We could go to the islands,
the netherworld full of coral,
and have our portraits painted
in feathers and mud—I know this betokens
a kinship too rickety, or even sizzling, for you.
Mammoths walked there a decade ago,
lonely, tottering along the channels.
They looked at their thumbs and shrugged.
They took out their brains and hurled them
into the reefs. I'm holding a crust of bread
in my palm, I see our initials rising
from the lithosphere, a couple of pinpoints
of utility needed elsewhere, and I remember
how to cry, and I remember you, my last kin.

II

If you look a dog
in the eye
too intently,
it may recite
an astounding poem
to you.

—Jean Genet,
Funeral Rites

Trying to Help

On another planet, a silvery starlet is brooding
on her salary. Some gangling ranchers are blindfolding her
for her own good, or so they say. It's all part of some lawful
research, or maybe they said "awful research," I wasn't listening.
I was roving down a chestnut lane, thinking about origins
in a contrite sort of way, amid the nearly inaudible society
of aphids and such, modulating my little hireling feet
none too carefully, an average stroller praying for keepsakes,
or at least one, when I heard this eerie squeak from afar.
For reasons which I refuse to explain I knew instantly
what was going on, and I tried to negotiate in my rudimentary way.
I offered up some rose petals, I think they were tempted
but liked playing tough because it was in their contract
or something. So I offered to play the fiddle on their patio
for a whole night. No deal—I don't think they knew what a fiddle was,
which was actually lucky for me since I have but one tiny tune.
I sat down on my chestnut lane, tempted to sneer at my own timidity.
Those squeaks from afar, all that damned distant research,
provide the only keepsake for this day, my momentum crushed.
Hours pass, crows pass, a pheasant crashes into an oak tree.
In a dream she says to me, "Thanks for caring, mister,
but it's all part of the plot, and I'm getting paid awfully well."
And now I can hardly walk.

How Was Your Day?

After a morning of miniature golf,
everything everything seemed smaller.
The cardplayers at the club—tiny.
And what I wanted most was grandeur!
So I checked into the Grand Hotel.
Things were beginning to turn around.
On an outing, I clambered up the tomb
of some monstrous dictator—feeling
really excellent now. I had tea
with several obese bluestockings,
a beer with an encyclopedist who himself
resembled a mosque. Some days nothing
arrives in its proper package, and
I hate that. There are the flattened bodies,
the diaphanous tabloids, the speckled sauces.
All I can do is clutch the phone in my Thinkery,
popping seedless grapes—poor seeds—
and in an almost devotional or neutral voice
I ask room service for an eagle sandwich—
I am suddenly suffocating—cancel that—
make that a knuckle sandwich, chopped lips—
oh, hell—please connect me with the horticulture
consultant standing this minute beneath the pyramids.
I'm checking out, I'm going home to my little bungalow—
actually, it's the perfect size. I'm going to kneel down
on the veranda and toss kisses at the setting sun.
On the horizon, a pregnant woman blots out the sun.
It's okay, I tell myself, since she herself is crimson.
Chopped lips, nodding off in a life of perpetual learning.
Tranquility weaves its dim web around my imperfect rags.

A Complicated and Petty Set of Procedures in a Single Room

Perched on the edge of my bed
(which is shaped like a Trident submarine),
I am serenading some amphibia
who just dropped in, they want to classify me
as a fern, when clearly the opposite is true:
I'm a depleted industrialist eating his porridge,
I have a brunette babysitter in the toilet
who will be back any minute with something frozen
that can be slammed against a lamp,
we'll be fondling a lot and then telephoning
old factories along the palisades, now
with lips closed. Her belly will redden
like certain upholstery, and maybe then she'll
need to call her guidance counsellor,
and I'll still be sitting here like a borrowed statue,
and the nosy amphibia will suddenly be interested in
all things Japanese—who could blame them?—
and I'll press the buzzer and marionettes
will descend from the ceiling and entertain me,
motionless, for what seems like an eternity.
I didn't blink at all, but I did squint.
I felt some kind of brackets closing in around me.
The washbowl was a thousand miles away.
The room was beginning to slope,
a huge bowl of steaming gumbo slid by.
The babysitter—we'll call her Wendy—
lithe, angular, comes wheeling out of the anti-room—
a windswept gossamer with an armload of projectiles
accusing me of gobbling the banquet
and exposing the mummies in my dangling solitude.
She's right, of course, but still, she doesn't even exist.

Moving

After slogging quadrillion kilometers
they were susurrating into one another's
eardrums: ". . . petrified . . . I'm leaking . . .
the thermometer, please." Plovers
scattered up from a thornbush and a dead fly
whizzed by. "Perhaps we'll find a telephone
soon, but they (who are *they*?) might mistake us
for escaped prisoners. . . ." Her voice faltering,
her bosom . . . An eruption nearby
silenced them. A monastery disappeared
into the earth. Someone shouted "Goodbye!"
Now all was barren before them, except
for one duplex with a wagon on its lawn,
and some honeysuckle blooming beside both doors,
and a creek by the side with some minnows splashing around;
and there were eleven spoons lined-up on the sidewalk.
Melody thought this was a poignant display,
perhaps designed to welcome them back
from their quadrillion kilometers, but
she didn't want to be guilty of reading into things
at this point, especially since Franklin
had just unpacked his portable footstool
and was now mechanically scratching himself all over
and she knew he could become peevish
at this hour of the afternoon. Perhaps
this was where they were to live from now on,
she with her embroidery, and he gluing something
back together again, an astonishing geometry
of the everlasting, the eleven utensils
all lined up and ready to go. She curled
her arms around herself. A latchkey was gnawing
its way toward them, humming a love song
about dumplings, or dimples, or deformity.

Such long journeys usually end in proneness
or mutiny, Franklin was thinking
while rolling a straw from side to side in his mouth.
Melody was going to name their kitten "Whorls."
She wondered why it was a duplex, though,
and not a single-family dwelling.

Horse Gets Dark

Out of the crevices of our predilections
animalcules begin a recital, boisterous
as sharecroppers, disarming the cucumber
salad of its windchime and coat-hanger.
I taste my own medicine, my mouthful of salt.
There is the placemat, the silverware,
a waterstain on our prayerbook.
I've a nickel in my pocket that can buy joy!
I had to cross a footbridge, I was on my way
to the hospital. Marigolds near the faucet
like the campfires of yesteryear:
your life is a snowball to the heart!
I dream the same as you: horse gets dark.
And the horse gets darker. The moon spills
beans into your open hands, short of a picnic.
On the other side there was a small auction
of watercolors by my sick friend.

Pastoral

With lukewarm tongs I hold this swaying cow.
She's dripping cubes into the cove below.
And little Hank fills his glass and blows
the bubbles in my face and I laugh: ho ho . . .
O blissful, plump swimmer in Life's disfigured
crossword, don't frown. I'll set you down
unchurned-up. Now you're happy and dumb
and Hank can dip his donut in the wind . . .
A hooded figure slithers by, an oblong reptile
with dahlias for eyes. I pause, curse, and bend,
pick up a squeezed-out tube of something blue.
The hooded figure sneezes. "Kazoontite," I say.
"Well, I guess I'll be moseying back to the barn.
If I don't get back soon I'll miss the Farm Report."
"Is that you in there, Ma," little Hank detected.
"You sure scared Pa, fooled him good this time."
This farm-funning is going to give me a nervous
breakdown. And I suppose this squeezed-out tube
of blue means something, too, like bald-faced
vexation. The hooded one shakes her beak: yes.

Aunt Sophie's Morning

A spinster swats a worm on her tabletop.
It was heading for the waffles or the coffee.
She's read about this in the tabloids, oceanic
worms with nerve systems like radio signals.
They are blind as icepicks and don't care.
They come in the morning when you're barely awake
and carve their initials on tabletops.
Maybe you pick one up thinking it's a lipstick.
Maybe they are in the bathtub with you.
Or maybe they just curl up in the fireplace
and shine until your favorite cat is legally dead.
They're not bad worms, she says, they're just different.

Nuisance

It was more of a nuisance
than an actual apparition.
It wanted my microfilm, it
was spraying me with an atomizer
such as one I had never seen.
I even carried an umbrella around
inside the house for a while.
I sat in my armchair with
a saucer of warm milk and took
my temperature several times.
I calculated some errors
I had made in recent days,
all the while this tingling
at my temples, as though I were
being spied on by satellites,
as though some inscrutably virulent
sanitation problem were attacking
my very foundation, and hecklers
were arriving by the busloads.
I tried yawning—it was broken.
I could tidy up a bit, pad
from room to room, polish
the corroding molecular remnants.
After all, it's just so much propaganda,
really, it's nothing more than a massive
injection of disembodied transparencies
on a simple excursion, a vacation,
brief, in all likelihood, millimeter
by millimeter subtracting my formulas,
maiming a few of my components.
But, then again, I saw nothing.
I could hardly be called a witness.

The Banner

I tugged at her sleeve: *doorbell*?
She hugged the arm: *magpie*.
Intervals went by spotlessly,
but somehow foetid, too. She stitched,
I read the Apocrypha, abruptly slammed
shut the covers, suspicious
of fumes rippling through the room.
I was poking around under cushions,
bracing myself for the worst, dead
fruit, something under the rug,
a gelatinous potato. *Would you stop*?
she pleaded. *I'm cooking*. *Oh,* I said,
that explains everything. I stared at her
for a very long time, I felt horns
growing, meagre horns denting my baldspot.
That book was a fake, a neon sneer
across the ages, a prolonged rasp
corrupting the squeamish, among whom
I loomed as a negligible connoisseur.
I felt discouraged now as I watched
her leathery fingers unfold
her munificent banner: *Endurance,*
it read, as though the Bridegroom
had endowed her, and she were the Bride?
I tugged at her sleeve: *telephone*?
She rocked in her trance: *coyotes*.

Foreign Airport

Moonlight keeps popping into the hypochondriac's head.
And yet it is barely noon. A mule is silhouetted
on the runway—he's a hybrid going nowhere. A school-
master offers peanuts to a bailbondsman—they discover
they are both Geminis, both born in Lemon, South Dakota,
on the same day, minutes apart, indeed, they are twins!
They make unconvincing pledges to stay in touch, and
the conversation drifts, like the aroma of a shipwreck
bisecting a heartbeat in bathwater. A stewardess with
a hairdo from hell is complaining of the crummy casino—
"Cheapskate syphilitics!" The bartender smiles and raises
his forefinger to his lips. There's a kind of permanent
prehistory here in the air, a carnivorous skeleton
burning windchimes in the corner. One doesn't age
in a place like this. We just wait, as in the hours before
combat, when neither this world nor the next matters,
thoughts agape, concealing the velocity of our fears,
until the handsome pilot arrives and anoints us with oil,
and we are airborne at last, putt-putting over this pale orchid.

Las Ramblas

The dove-venders were murmuring under their masks.
Two soldiers ambushed one another over some passing cleavage.
A rosary was said outside an unbuttoned saloon.
Sunbaked tarantulas paused to appraise the newest bowler hats;
they have escaped from a science project and are pretending
to tightrope-walk across the melting jewelry of the boulevard.
Crowds fish for money; salads are helicoptered in to restaurants,
icy claws hurl puppies in the air as a hoax; a séance is cancelled.
I am staring at my brochure, which way is up? The labyrinth
rhythmically monotones directions to an olive tree, is this it?
Are we there yet? I peek into a keyhole: a slumbering maid
with her bonnet cocked and her tongue lapping her forehead.
I'm spellbound by this tableau of repose, but it's back
into the street for me, bumped hither and thither, toppled
by lopsided cadavers, briskly converging only to dump me
into the cooing shade of the dove-venders' rivalry, where
I sleep like a baby in the soothing orchard of my brochure.

Ebb

A mountaineer and a dentist were placing cheesecloth
over their thing. It was frosty out, though they both
were sleeveless. I was thumbing through my stamp album,
sipping something smooth on my ancient mattress, something
greenish, dabbling at psychic research, fingering
my harmonica, remembering a few Psalm fragments.
The dentist was looking doubtfully at a handful of chunky
crystals—I think he is an orphan—I saw him in a newsreel
during the long summer of '58—; he hands them to the mountaineer—
who feels invaded, motherless. And there could be a windstorm
coming any minute now, I feel its electricity rising in my veins.
All of us will be completely varnished, I mean drenched.
The wagons should be closing, we should be cooperating.
It is impossible to duplicate the potroast I had before leaving.
We are completely exposed, like a rabbi facing a stork—
I mean, there's this inanimate thinness in the tremors,
and the bestowing of the crystals makes me want to cry
as if I myself had thrown a pet goose out the porthole
just as the situation, usually so diverting, was now
ushering in the dismaying, leprous, sustained smallness
prayed for but forgotten in our grandfather's last days.

We Go a-Quilting

From the quagmire, several heathens
were tooting their investment plans.
There was a piazza not far away, and
they dreamed of pistol-whipping a missionary
or a chemist, or just splashing around
anonymously and doing their homework
behind a vehicle made of lace which
would vibrate beneath them like a stallion
devoted to his own misbehavior. Such
were their thoughts: bad business
reminded them of how unattractive and
indispensable were the spasms of their
deaf leader—oh, he had his insomnia,
he too was subjected to the dressmaker's
whims, the preambles, the detours,
the historical bandits. Her ten-thousand
scraps squeezed into the cave and the slumped
leaders lecturing on obedience, and the stern
doctrines which are the archenemy
of the truth. But there was still room
for a threadlike caper, like a gabardine cicada
balancing in the niche between this chasm
and that nocturne. There was a spectre
wailing somewhere, and it made them happy
to be alive, even as authentic poverty
transforms this world into a rose
no one can any longer recognize.

Editor

It was a foggy day anyway,
and my cockatoo was scorched,
and my bikini was moping in the ruins,
so I started reading a journal some poky guy had written
and dropped on my doorstep disguised
in a baboon uniform. The rhythms
were all crooked, and he seemed to live
at the margins, outcast even by himself,
snatching limps from the vast gaps
and presuming to slip through checkpoints
with official documents stuffed in his bloodshot eyeballs,
when, in fact, the hatcheck girl's own torpor
beheld the preposterous sloth with pinched nostrils.
He claims he was born with thirteen digits.
Years later he pirated a schooner
and sailed it over a waterfall.
He was in London during the blitz.
He lived on crayfish alone in a swamp for seven years.
Then he procured white women for a famous eastern emperor.
He was implicated in an assassination plot
and has been working at a school crossing since.
He feels the time has come to tell his story.
I feel some old shrapnel crawling around in my head.
I want fresh bandages. I want to shoot out his stoplight.

Indivisible

Some genetic prodding in the termite's nest,
accomplished by servants with arrows,
led to some dodgy sandwiches in the pet shop.
I was yelping with a pitchfork at some gummy weathervane.
Predatory delicacies were sifting through the cradle.
I assigned myself the task of pasting up itineraries for the victims.
Once in a motel I put some electrodes on a chimp,
I'm sorry about that. I turned newts into astronauts,
that was a mistake. Maybe my cousin is a dolphin, I don't know.
There are networks of cells that form sponges
on which this galaxy exists. Their urgent criteria
woven into the buffeting, if feeble, sensory geometry
of woebegone trains, emulating distinct convenience.
It's the maintenance of hierarchies that breaks our backs.
I find peace in lava, in plums, in kernels with exact instructions.
I am hushed when it comes to an arsenal of viscera,
I am piqued when the soggy grasp at me in tubs.
I provide, casually; incidentally, I partake.
I have sampled some devotions, I have envisioned being
perpetually hitched. I have set myself on fire with kerosene.
And now I walk among my town's folk, immune, beseeching.

If you are chosen
town clerk,
forsooth, you cannot go to
Tierra del Fuego
this summer:
but you may go
to the land of infernal fire
nonetheless.

—Henry Thoreau

I Am a Finn

I am standing in the post office, about
to mail a package back to Minnesota, to my family.
I am a Finn. My name is Kasteheimi (Dewdrop).

Mikael Agricola (1510–1557) created the Finnish language.
He knew Luther and translated the New Testament.
When I stop by the Classé Café for a cheeseburger

no one suspects that I am a Finn.
I gaze at the dimestore reproductions of Lautrec
on the greasy walls, at the punk lovers afraid

to show their quivery emotions, secure
in the knowledge that my grandparents really did
emigrate from Finland in 1910—why

is everyone leaving Finland, hundreds of
thousands to Michigan and Minnesota, and now Australia?
Eighty-six percent of Finnish men have blue

or grey eyes. Today is Charlie Chaplin's
one hundredth birthday, though he is not
Finnish or alive: "Thy blossom, in the bud

laid low." The commonest fur-bearing animals
are the red squirrel, muskrat, pine-marten
and fox. There are about 35,000 elk.

But I should be studying for my exam.
I wonder if Dean will celebrate with me tonight,
assuming I pass. Finnish literature

really came alive in the 1860s.
Here, in Cambridge, Massachusetts,
no one cares that I am a Finn.

They've never even heard of Frans Eemil Sillanpää,
winner of the 1939 Nobel Prize in Literature.
As a Finn, this infuriates me.

I Am Still a Finn

I failed my exam, which is difficult
for me to understand because I am a Finn.
We are a bright, if slightly depressed, people.

Pertti Palmroth is the strongest name
in Finnish footwear design; his shoes and boots
are exported to seventeen countries.

Dean brought champagne to celebrate
my failure. He says I was just nervous.
Between 1908 and 1950, 33 volumes

of The Ancient Poetry of the Finnish People
were issued, the largest work of its kind
ever published in any language.

So why should I be nervous? Aren't I
a Finn, descendant of Johan Ludvig Runeberg
(1804–1877), Finnish National poet?

I know he wrote in Swedish, and this
depresses me still. Harvard Square
is never "empty." There is no chance

that I will ever be able to state honestly
that "Harvard Square is empty tonight."
A man from Nigeria will be opening

his umbrella, and a girl from Wyoming
will be closing hers. A Zulu warrior
is running to catch a bus and an over-

painted harlot from Buenos Aires will
be fainting on schedule. And I, a Finn,
will long for the dwarf birches of the north

I have never seen. For 73 days the sun
never sinks below the horizon. O
darkness, mine! I shall always be a Finn.

The Expert

talks on and on.
At times he seems lost
in his own personal references,
to be adrift in a lonely pleasure craft.
He has spent his life collecting evidence,
and now it is oozing away down the aisles
of indifferent eavesdroppers.
He spins and points out the window:
"There," he says passionately,
"that is what I mean."
We look: a squirrel flicks its tail and disappears.
His point made, the expert yawns
and we can see deep into his cavernous body.
We are impressed, but also frightened
because there appears to be a campfire
almost out of control on the left bank
of his cave. But then he is off
on one of his special obsessions
and we are back to feeling inferior
and almost nonexistent. We have never
even heard of this phenomenon:
how a thing can hurt and still
grow that fast until it walks off
the map and keep growing while
falling through space. We want
to pinch ourselves, but softly
and slowly. Who among us
invited this expert? He is pacing now
as though flirting with some edge
only he can see. Someone shouts
"Jump!" and he wakes again
and eyes us with suspicion,

and maybe we are guilty of something.
We have no idea what he has given
his life for, though I think
it has something to do with
a monster under the bed.
He is growing old before our eyes,
and no one can catch him now,
no one, that is, except his lost mother.

Vito Takes His Neighbor's Dog for a Drive

A woodpecker is duplicating hell-bent stitches
and, in the ravine, a ballet dancer is slithering toward a bunch
    of onions.
Vito stands by the heaving cedars and watches a salad
parachute into a trapeze net.

He remembers a sexual encounter in a janitor's closet
in an airport, zone of shelves darting into a beige milestone,
a cactus repulsing its own penumbra,
spun sugar slouching around without a vocation.

She said: "I don't care how I feel about being an angel
without a muddy carcass clattering around
in fluffiness without shoestrings or flippers."

Later, she said: "I might like being a nail driven into a cameo,
or calling Charlotte Brontë collect in the middle of the night."

Vito returned, after an absence of seven years.
His neighbor's dog was restless and wanted to join the rodeo.
Something happened in the night—two pterodactyls
were circling—a man was flying to Pakistan
to meet his mother after eight years—chewing gum—
the statistics, bellowing, the statistics, a fire—

a newborn calf, full of pride and fierce hunger, leapt—
and that's when Vito had had enough. He dressed,
very deliberately, with the firm knowledge
that his sole duty at this hour—to tap out an existence
within these flames—was to drive drive and drive
that neighbor's dog around the world.

Crimes Against the Lyric

She throws her ragdoll to within earshot
of a viola and, miles downstream,
a gramophone loses power.
There is a cooing from the mountaintop.
Bees have been struck by lightning.
A looking-glass is hurled down in self-defense.
The multitudinousness of the world
stops her from having one clean thought.
She hauls her ball of darkness
through the cardboard town,
it's condemned reality, windy memos,
flat wisdom. She dreams
through vital negotiations
older than this world.
A mailman thinks about jumping,
then jumps a little.
A tobacco barn for one minute
truly believes it has grown a steeple.

Poem

The angel kissed my alphabet,
it tingled like a cobweb in starlight.
A few letters detached themselves
and drifted in shadows, a loneliness
they carry like infinitesimal coffins
on their heads.

She kisses my alphabet
and a door opens: blackbirds roosting
on far ridges. A windowpeeper
under an umbrella watches
a funeral service. Blinkered horses
drum the cobblestones.

She kisses: Plunderers gather
in a lackluster ballroom
to display their booty. Mice
testify against one another
in dank rodent courtrooms.

The angel kisses my alphabet,
she squeezes and bites,
and the last lights flutter,
and the violins are demented.
Moisture spreads across my pillow,
a chunk of quartz thirsts
to abandon my brain trust.

No Spitting Up

"People in glass elevators shouldn't carry snow shovels,"
I said to Sheila, because we were in one with a lady who was.
I faced the closed doors, rejected the view of the city
without the slightest curiosity, because I already knew.
What if this woman with the shovel suddenly went crazy,
started flapping her wings like a chicken, like a fiend?
I wonder what Sheila is thinking just now, I wonder if she
has her eye on the snow shovel, how it can't rest
in this glass elevator, how it is dancing inside of itself
and making me dance. No one's paying the least attention
to the tension between me and that shovel, that shovel
and that window, that window and me.

The Less Said

The parents of the deceased
studied his calligraphy endlessly.
Once at a card game at Furzy Park
the father, Mr. Nobody, squealed,
"Looky here! he was just a May fly
and therefore lived a full life."
A meteorite went by a second later
and he said, "Or a meterorite, and
he lived a full, a magnificent life."
"But what about his calligraphy?"
asked their hosts, Don and Dorothy.
Mrs. Nobody, hoping for a thunderbolt,
or at least for a petal to fall, murmured,
"It was real steamy, like boiling milk.
That child was nothing more than a
silhouette of a geyser, if you ask me.
But we miss him, don't we, Harry?"
And that's when Harry said, "The less said."

An Extraterrestrial

The meteorite tore red sashes in the nightsky.
(I was a small, hungry thing running around
with my pain and my little bag of joy.)
It sped on to meet its appointment
in Weathersford, Connecticut, right through
the roof and onto the living-room floor,
the six pounds of it four billion years old,
object of nameless gasses and minerals
silencing the argument of Mr. and Mrs. Boyd.

All those days when nothing happened!

And then, at least, the visit,

and the struggle to surrender.

Black Monday

As a specimen I was determined to get back
to the fancy little cove and spare the rabbit
his immediate spearing. And now when I allude
to a certain insubstantial cove and a rabbit
that was speared there not long ago, everyone
believes me. I describe a windmill and a pine tree,
the coat I was wearing, and the tailor who made it,
his horrible death in the granary. I darted
under the shelves and began to itemize
the contingencies: the alleged commerce, the botany
of it all. In short, I've been a passenger hovering
over the Japanese. I yearned for all things Japanese.
I had rendered the leaves and was about to parachute.
In a small, plastic cabin nearby, a pointillist
was melting his crayons in the fireplace.
As a specimen I have avoided beige slippers.
The rabbit was locked up in a welcome wagon,
or was he faking his imprisonment because
in his heart he is a scumbucket? A Japanese?

Anatomy

The beautiful one studies anatomy
from dawn to dusk and then just sits there crying.
No one speaks to her in a friendly manner.
They know she is dying inside,
they can see it in her beautiful face.
They exchange glances that say "It won't be long now.
Soon we'll have this city back to ourselves
and our ugliness will become the standard."
But the beautiful one must walk the streets
to escape her mirrors, and she must read
her anatomy book in the park under the maple tree
to understand the looks the others give her.
She needs love, she tries to approach them with kindness,
with a smile and a kind word, but they shuffle past her
growling, their faces stuffed down into their overcoats.
She is shunned in the little vegetable store,
she is shunned in the museum, and in the church.
The beautiful one is dying, all alone,
no merciful words, no soft touch, no flowers.
Perhaps the city will be a better place to visit,
I don't know.

Beaucoup Vets

The soldier with a chicken up his ass,
the soldier with a chest full of balloons,
the soldier, the soldier back home
among the defenseless practitioners
of dead mall worship . . .

Taxidermy

The pastel bees I found in my mattress
really belong to the gravedigger. I was swallowing
my pencil down at headquarters when a meatloaf
crept out of the encyclopedia; it was shaped
like a chicken wearing a tiara but sinking in quicksand.
I hate this job, it's murder. The profile of a horse,
even a champion, can get rabbity, if the knitting needle
slips just a little. Thereupon my tranquilizer takes effect
and wrinkles disappear as if on a sailboat,
a twelve-inch one, and waterspouts bicycle around
like rodents plowing trenches, their equipment
concealed at night under the stairwell.
I'm all thumbs now. I get pregnant
squeezing my thumbs through buttonholes.
I'd like an atrocity to happen
just so I could enjoy the autumnal spice.
Everything is dead anyway, this mouse.
The squad on the beach stuffs my laundress.
Hitherto, the cameras of perdition crackling
as at an auction: How much for that one?
Will it last my lifetime?
Will it fade?

Haunted Aquarium

A white pigeon is digging for something in the snow.
As it digs further, it is disappearing.
A young girl finds it in the Spring,
a handkerchief of thin bones,
or a powder-puff she carries in her purse
for the rest of her days. Toward the end,
she gives it to her granddaughter,
who immediately recognizes it as the death
of the grandmother herself,
and flings it out the window.
It takes flight, utterly thankful
to feel like its old self again.
For a few precious moments it flies
in circles, then back in the window.
The grandmother pitches forward, dead.
The granddaughter lugs her toward the window:
Adieu! Godspeed!

She and the pigeon talk long into the night.

At breakfast, the grandmother says nothing.

About the author

James Tate grew up in Kansas City, Missouri. He is the author of *The Lost Pilot* (1967), *The Oblivion Ha-Ha* (1970), *Hints to Pilgrims* (1971), *Absences* (1972), *Viper Jazz* (1976), *Riven Doggeries* (1979), *Constant Defender* (1983), and *Reckoner* (1986). He teaches at the University of Massachusetts and lives in Amherst.

About the book

Distance from Loved Ones was composed on the Mergenthaler 202 in Galliard, a contemporary rendering of a classic typeface prepared for Mergenthaler in 1978 by the British type designer Matthew Carter. The book was composed by Brevis Press of Bethany, Connecticut, and designed and produced by Kachergis Book Design of Pittsboro, North Carolina.

Wesleyan University Press, 1990